Early Maths

Decimals

Just like a fraction, a decimal number represents the parts of a whole.

It consists of a dot between the digits in a number called decimal point.

As we move right from the decimal point, each place value is 1/10 (one tenth) the value of the number to its left.

Place value is the value of a digit according to its placement in the number.

For example

$\frac{9}{10} = 0.9$ → We read this number as nine tenths

Look at the following representation of a decimal with tenths.

Step 1

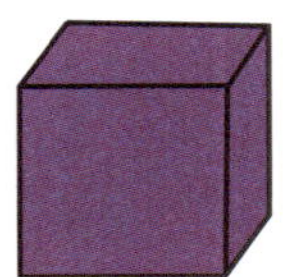

One (1) Whole unit

Step 2

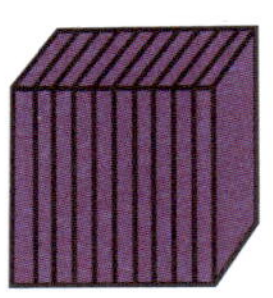

Split into ten equal parts (tenths)

Step 3

Each part is one tenth (0.1)

Write the fraction and decimal that represents the parts of the whole.

Blocks	Fraction	Decimal
	$\frac{1}{10}$	0.1 one tenth
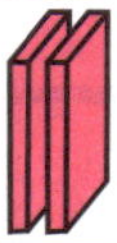	$\frac{2}{10}$	0.2 two tenths

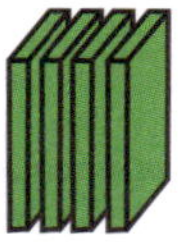		

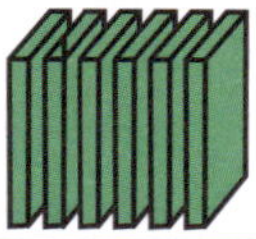		
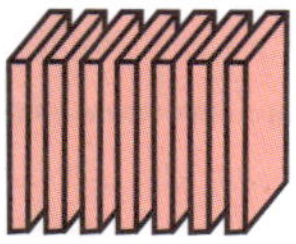		
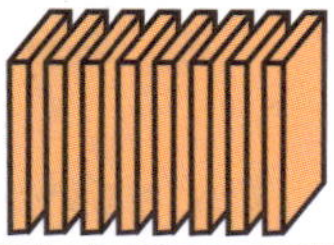		
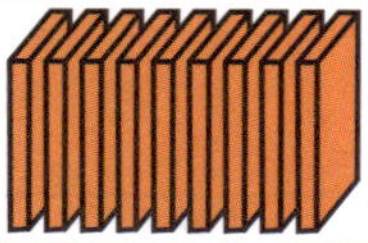		
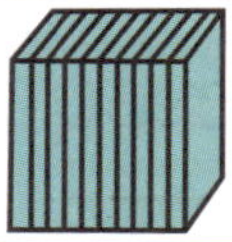	$\frac{10}{10}$	1 one
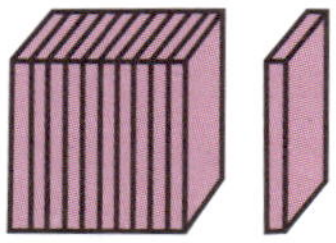	$1\frac{1}{10}$	1.1 one and one tenth
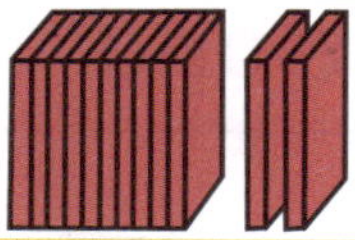		

Write the decimal number that the blocks represent in each of the following.

Write the following decimals in words. The first one has been done for you.

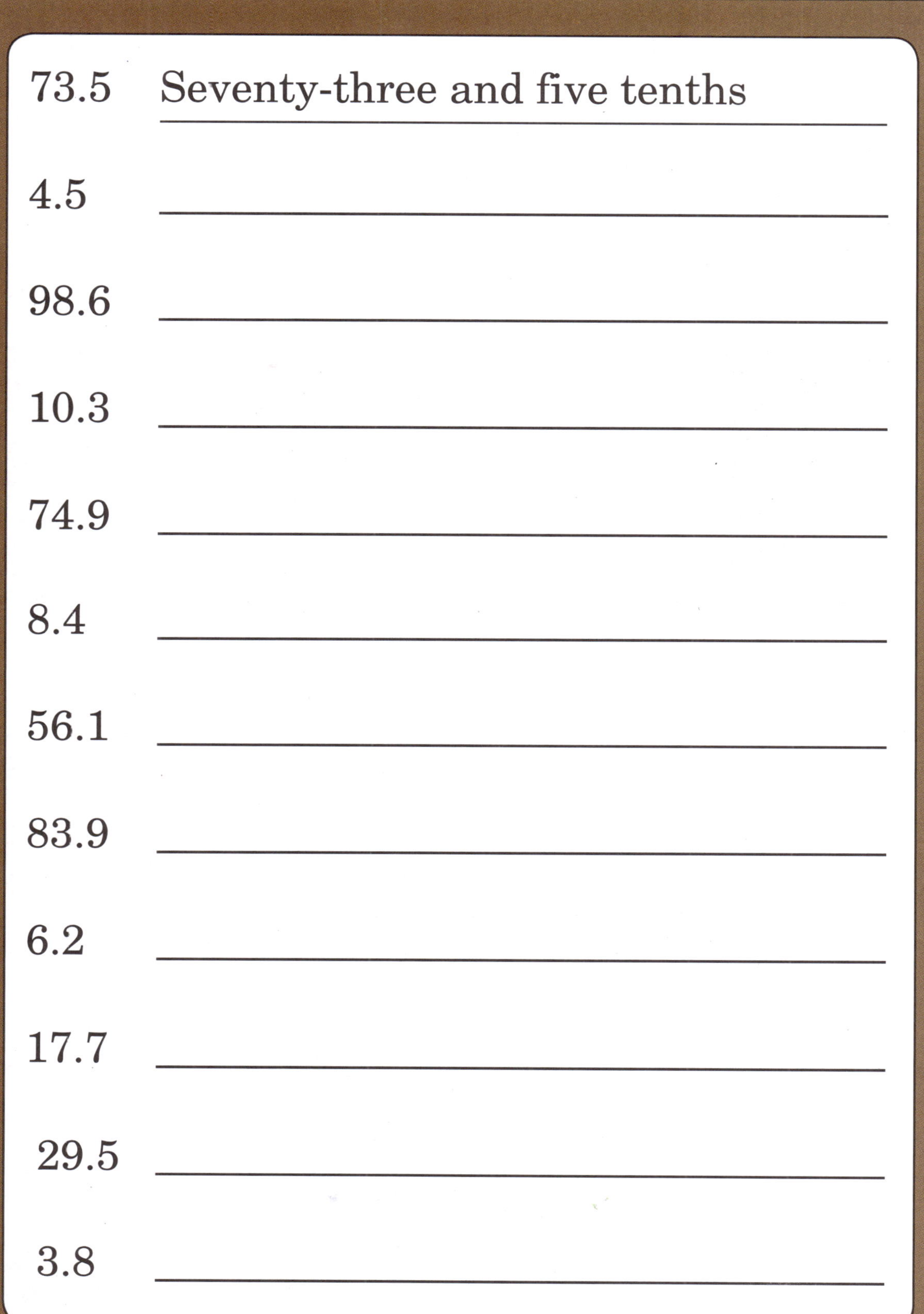

73.5 Seventy-three and five tenths

4.5 ______________________

98.6 ______________________

10.3 ______________________

74.9 ______________________

8.4 ______________________

56.1 ______________________

83.9 ______________________

6.2 ______________________

17.7 ______________________

29.5 ______________________

3.8 ______________________

Write the decimal represented by the coloured blocks.

(a) ______

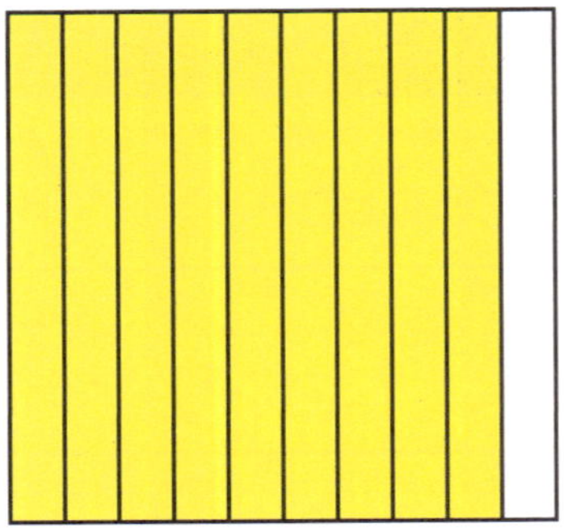

(b) ______

(c) ______

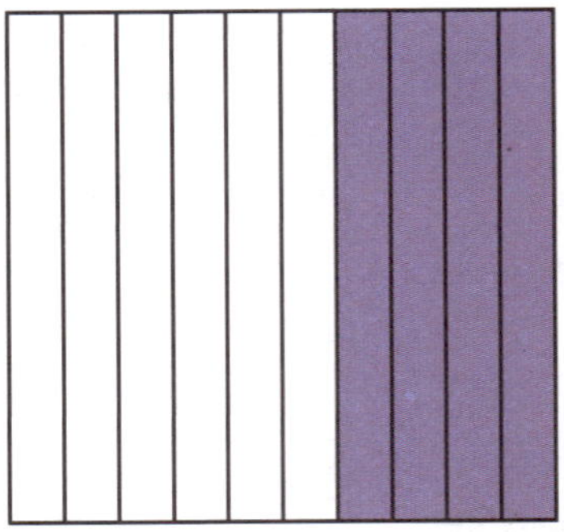

(d) ______

(e) ______

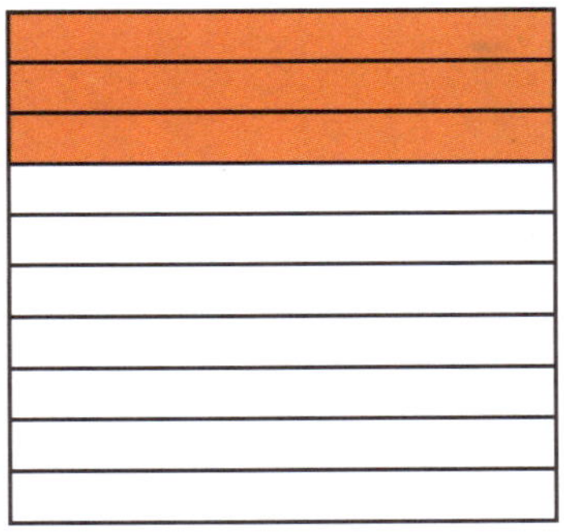

(f) ______

(g) ______

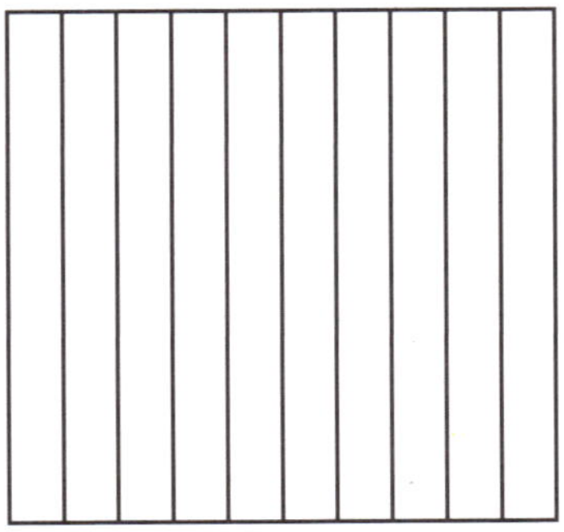

(h) ______

(i) ______

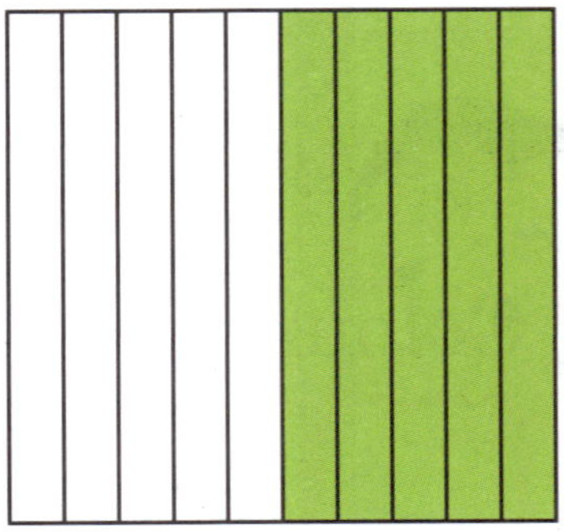

(j) ______

(k) ______

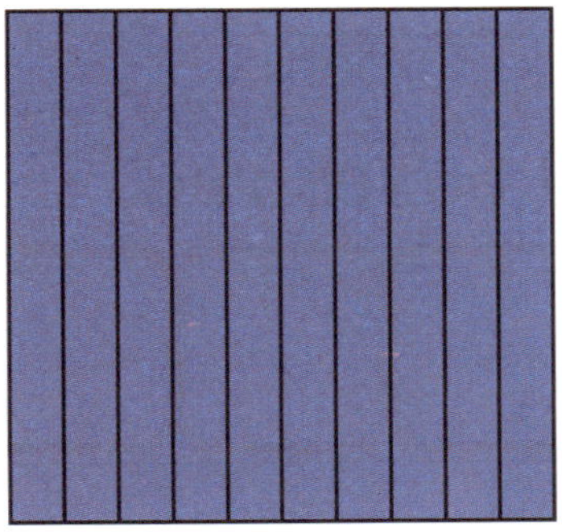

Follow the instructions and write the decimal and fraction accordingly.

Colour 8 out of 10 boxes red.

Fraction: ______________ Decimal: ______________

Colour 3 out of 10 boxes red.

Fraction: ______________ Decimal: ______________

Colour 7 out of 10 boxes red.

Fraction: ______________ Decimal: ______________

Colour 9 out of 10 boxes red.

Fraction: ______________ Decimal: ______________

Colour 6 out of 10 boxes red.

Fraction: ______________ Decimal: ______________

Identify and write decimals in hundredths. Some examples have been done for you.

One (1) whole unit

Split into ten equal parts (tenths - 0.1)

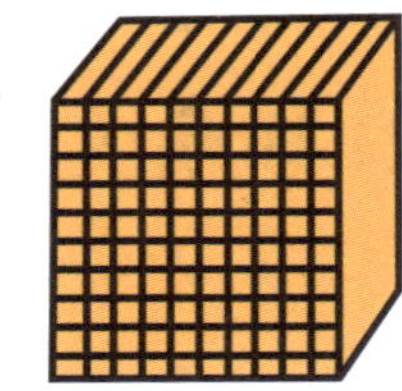

Each tenth split into ten equal parts

Each part is one hundredth (0.01)

Blocks	Fraction	Decimal
	$\frac{1}{100}$	0.01 one hundredth
	$\frac{2}{100}$	
	$\frac{44}{100}$	0.44 forty-four hundredths
	$\frac{35}{100}$	
	$1\frac{1}{100}$	1.01 one and one hundredths
	$1\frac{26}{100}$	1.26 one and twenty-six hundredths

Blocks	Decimal

Identify and write decimals in thousandths. Some examples have been done for you.

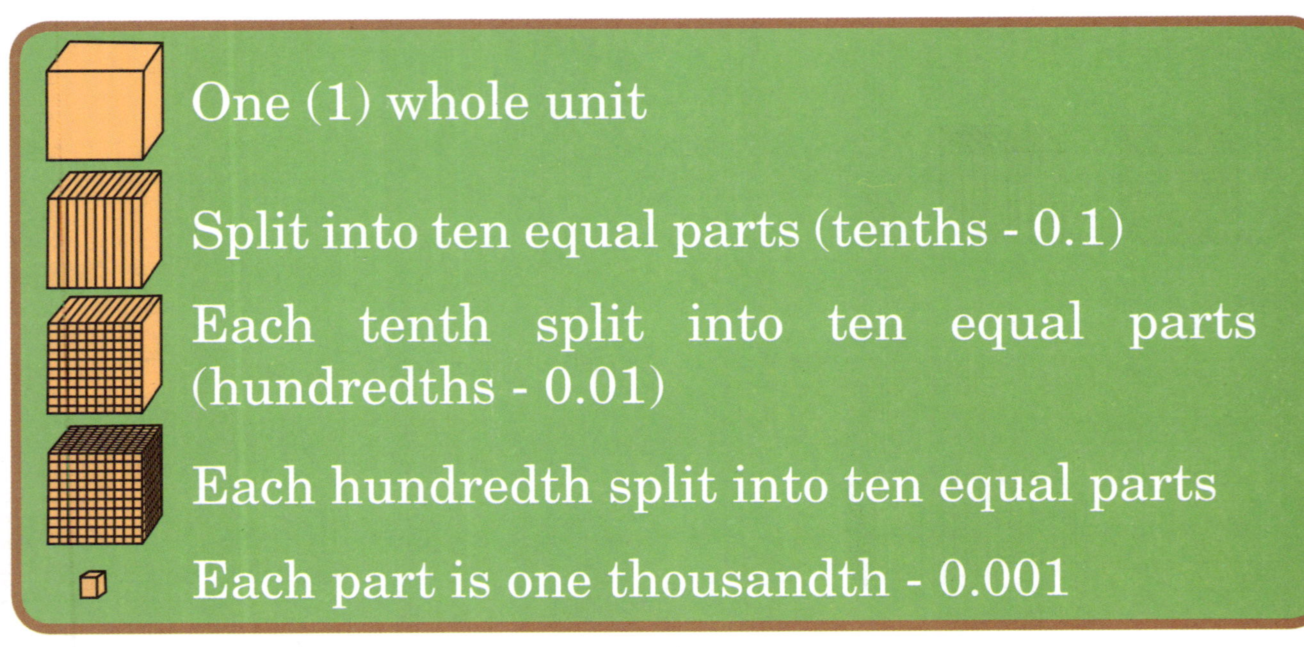

$\frac{1}{1000}$	0.001 one thousandth
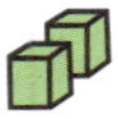 $\frac{2}{1000}$	
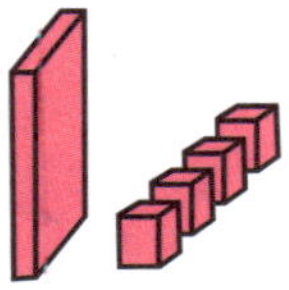 $\frac{104}{1000}$	0.104 one hundred four thousandths
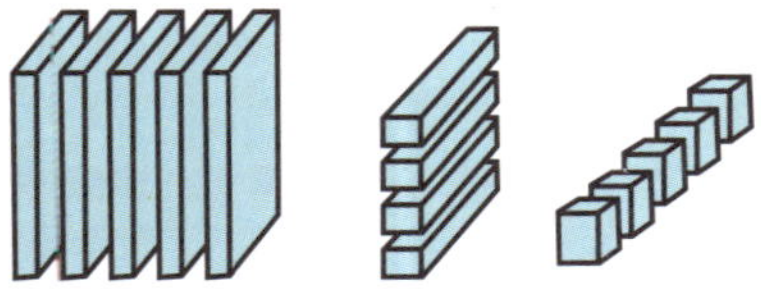 $\frac{545}{1000}$	
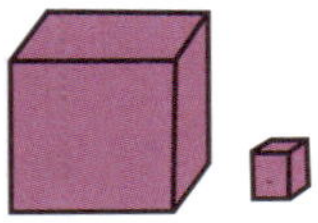 $1\frac{1}{1000}$	1.001 one and one thousandth

Blocks	Decimal
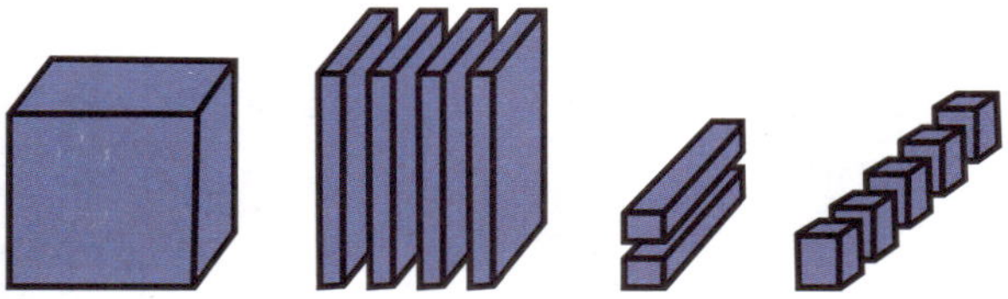	

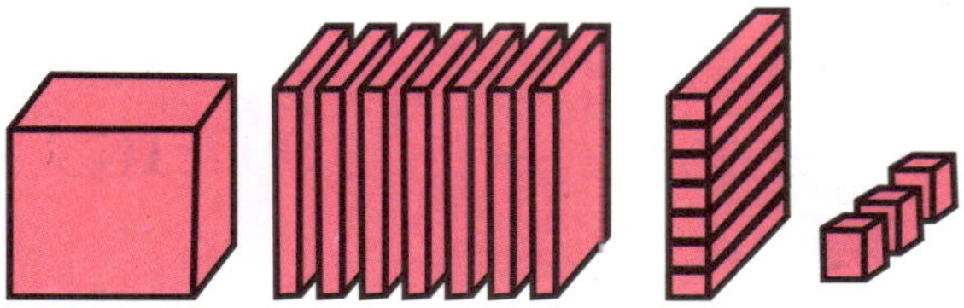	
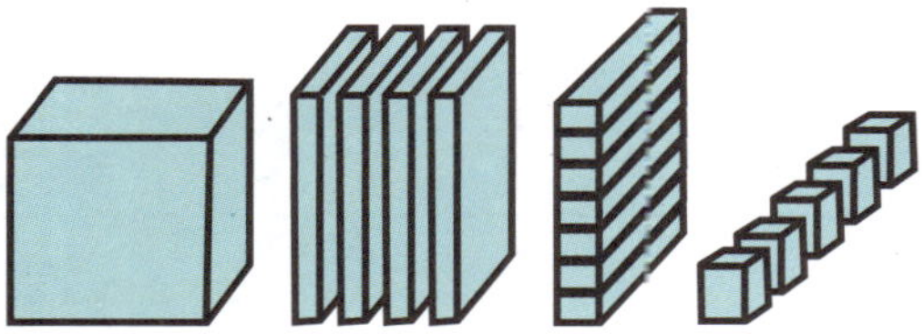	
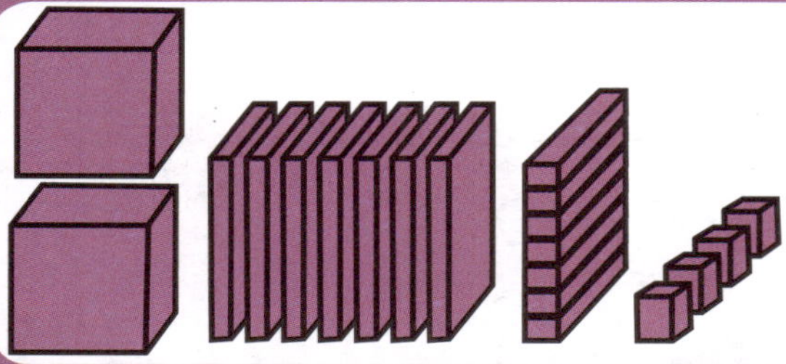	
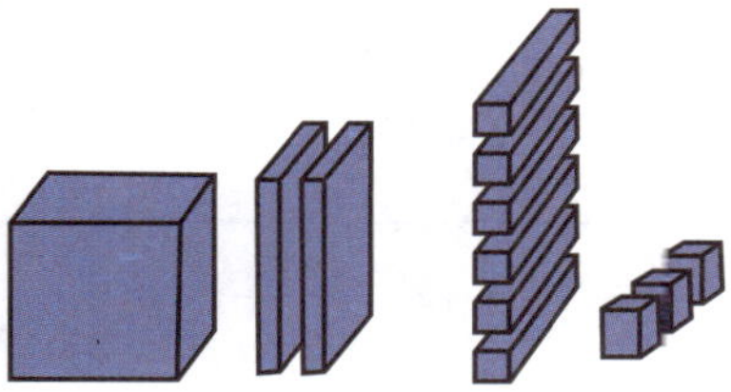	

Write the following decimal numbers in words.

8.44
18.27
5.99
335.72
79.03

When comparing decimals, start in the tenths place. The decimal with the biggest value is greater. Another way is to write the numbers in columns and add zeros to the right so that all the decimals have the same number of digits.

Example: 0.32, 0.9, 0.689, 1.56

0.32,		1.560,		
0.9,	→	0.900,	→	1.560 > 0.900 > 0.689 > 0.320
0.689,		0.689,		
1.56		0.320		

Order the decimals from the greatest to the smallest. One has been done for you.

0.8 > 0.4 > 0.1

0.13
0.98
0.20

0.92
0.11
0.15

0.31
0.19
0.43

0.38
0.89
0.73

0.09
0.68
0.24

0.45
0.92
0.42

0.61
0.82
0.30

0.94
0.30
0.12

Write the decimals in the descending order (greatest to smallest) . One has been done for you.

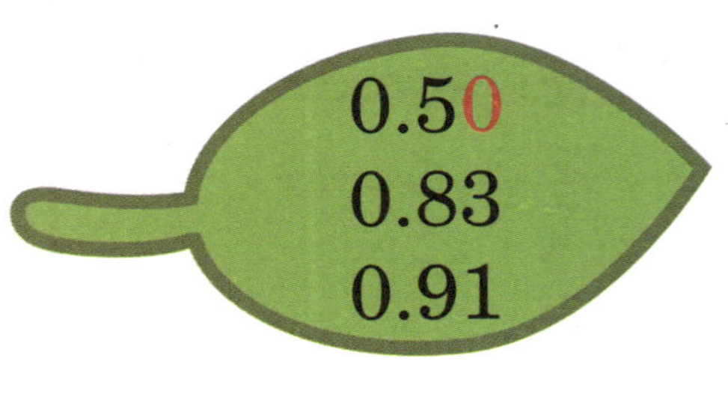

0.91 > 0.83 > 0.50

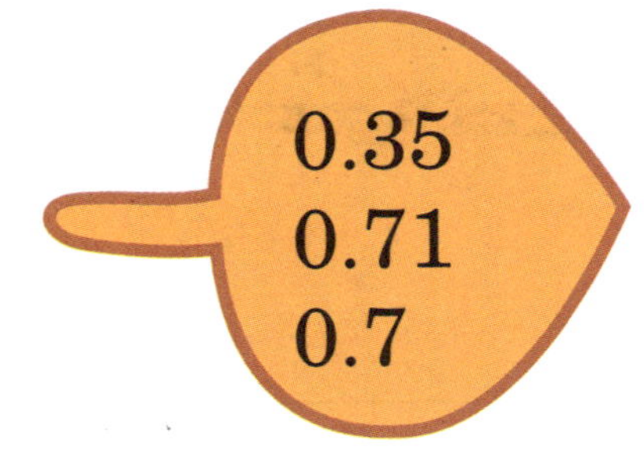

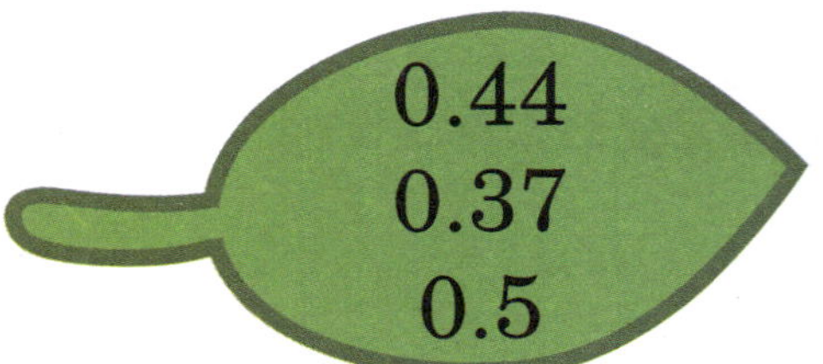

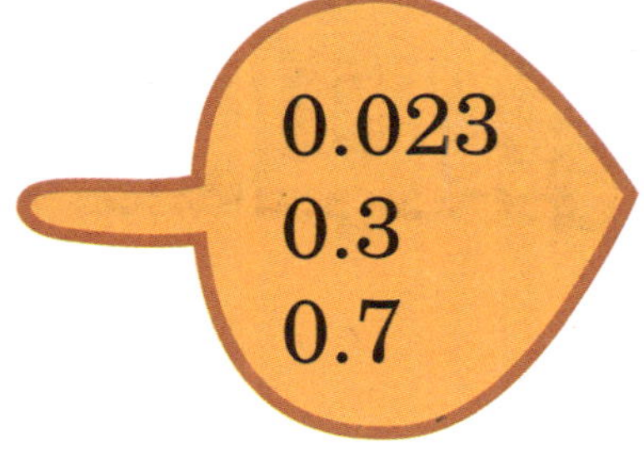

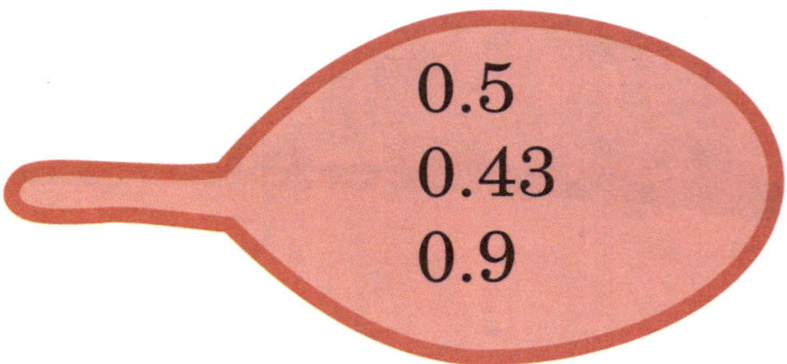

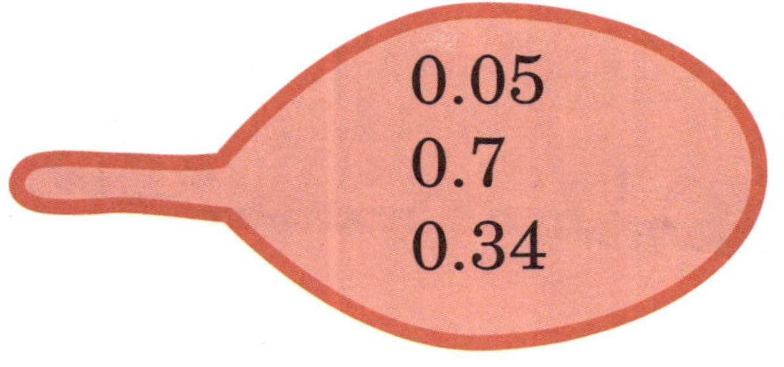

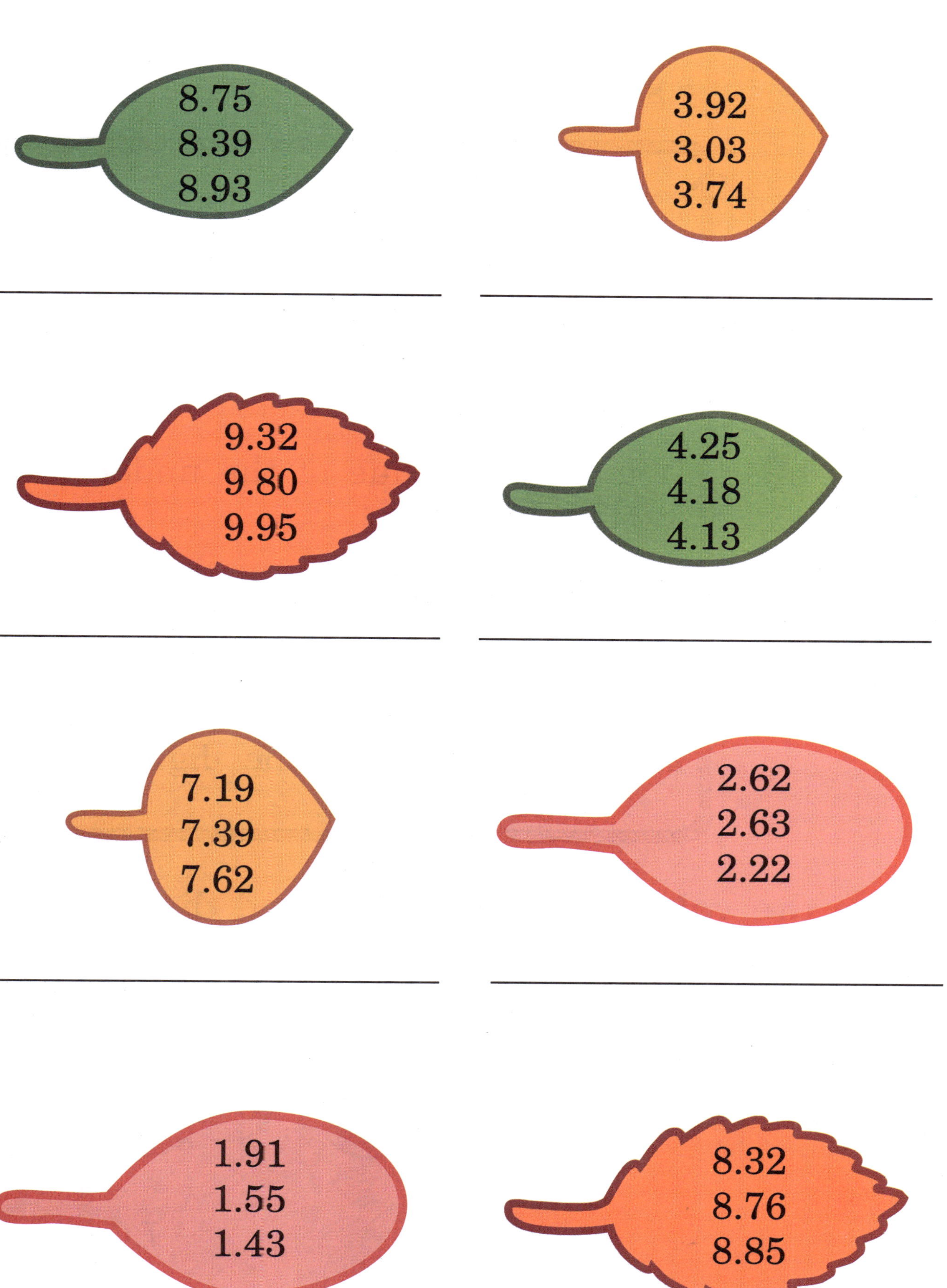
8.75
8.39
8.93
3.92
3.03
3.74
9.32
9.80
9.95
4.25
4.18
4.13
7.19
7.39
7.62
2.62
2.63
2.22
1.91
1.55
1.43
8.32
8.76
8.85

Look carefully at the given example and answer the questions given below.

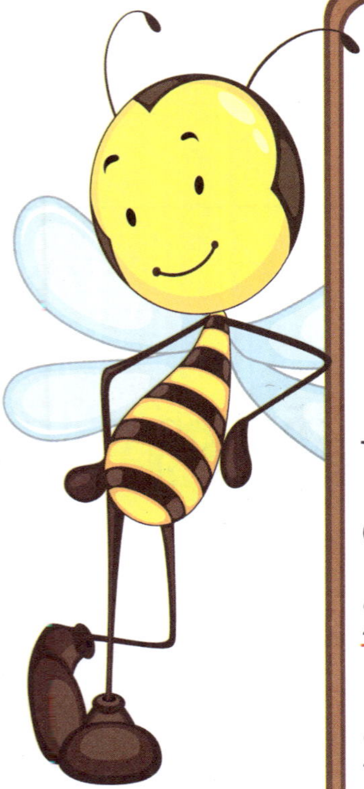

thousands, hundreds, tens, ones, tenths, hundredths, thousandths, ten thousandths

5, 1 3 4 . 4 3 2 1

Decimal point

What is the value of the underlined digit?

24.7 - The value of the digit 2 is 2 tens or 20.

24.7 - The value of the digit 4 is 4 ones, or 4.

24.7 - The value of the digit 7 is 7 tenths, or 0.7.

Write the values of the underlined digits. One has been done for you.

56.9 50	10.8 ________	46.4 ________
21.3 ________	4.5 ________	7.6 ________

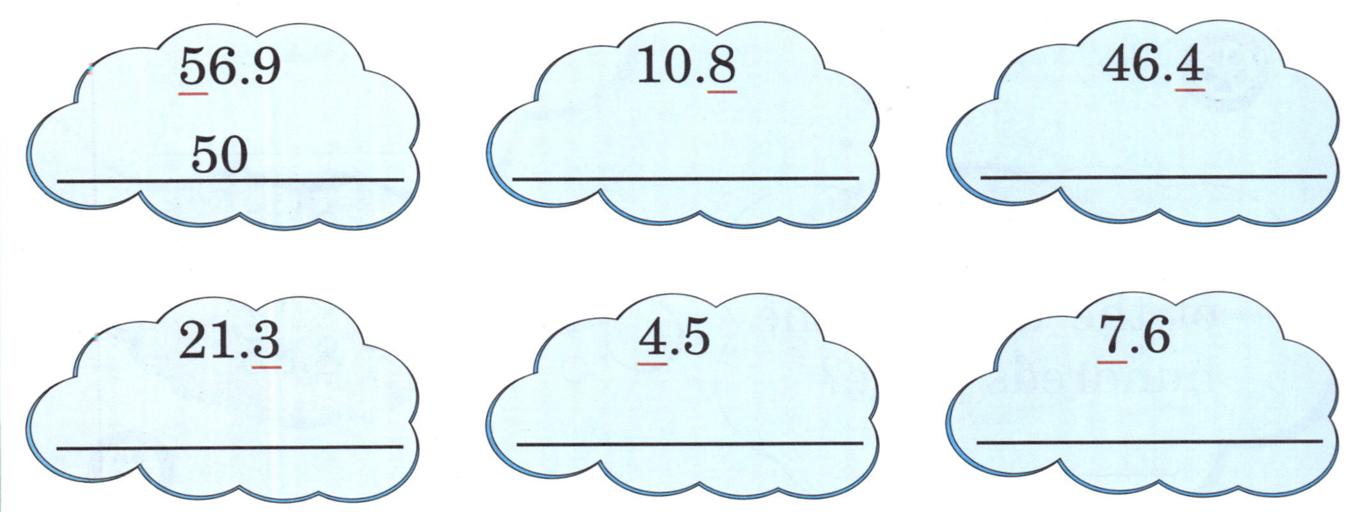

Answer the questions based on the given number.

1. Which digit has the greatest value?

____

2. Which digit has the least value?

____

3. What is the value of the digit in the tenths place?

____

4. What is the value of the digit in the ones place?

____

5. What is the value of the digit in the hundreds place?

____

Identify the decimal place value as asked. Circle your answer.

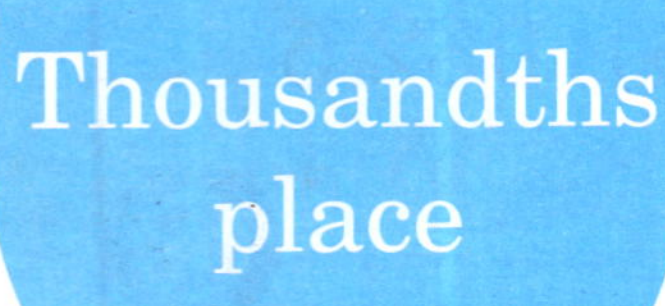

(a) 3.672 (b) 46.809

(c) 821.053 (b) 756.218

(a) 562.1 (b) 13.586

(c) 309.14 (d) 2.70

Hundreds place

(a) 823.40 (b) 261.349

(c) 197.8 (d) 594.1

(a) 235.46 (b) 423.16

(c) 86.357 (d) 5.2

Tens place

(a) 729.85 (b) 80.403

(c) 215.69 (d) 962.5

Thousandths place

(a) 2.674 (b) 387.215

(c) 54.362 (d) 92.561

(a) 76.943 (b) 123.567

(c) 67.208 (d) 5.829

(a) 12.896 (b) 3.602

(c) 742.93 (d) 473.529

Write the place value for the underlined digits in the following decimals. One has been done for you.

$83.5061\underline{7}6$ 0.00007 or 7 hundred thousandths

$7.14\underline{1}8$ ____________________

$931.\underline{8}1490$ ____________________

$6.3550\underline{1}$ ____________________

$42.923\underline{6}$ ____________________

$168.2\underline{7}051$ ____________________

$3.03\underline{2}789$ ____________________

953.2$\underline{1}$47 ____________________

24.037$\underline{6}$8 ____________________

8.1683$\underline{9}$0 ____________________

18.70$\underline{4}$6 ____________________

7.5$\underline{2}$1783 ____________________

346.$\underline{8}$902 ____________________

1.359$\underline{4}$8 ____________________

$\underline{7}$0.94683 ____________________

5.7615$\underline{3}$ ____________________

Choose the correct option. Read each question carefully and circle the right answer.

1. Circle the number in which 6 has the value 0.06

   (a) 132.4689 (b) 56.87

   (c) 20.637 (d) 641.9

2. Circle the number in which 3 has the value 0.3

   (a) 6.73120 (b) 734.095

   (c) 413.2 (d) 20.37

3. Circle the number in which 2 has the value 0.002

   (a) 8.7532 (b) 254.61

   (c) 19.3521 (d) 682.3

4. Circle the number in which 9 has the value 900

   (a) 2.19 (b) 906.8107

   (c) 836.9 (d) 679.512

5. Circle the number in which 4 has the value 0.0004

(a) 420.638 (b) 13.4

(c) 345.78 (d) 152.3614

6. Circle the number in which 5 has the value 0.5

(a) 685.132 (b) 870.59

(c) 45.2 (d) 38.65070

7. Circle the number in which 8 has the value 8

(a) 712.583 (b) 5.38

(c) 638.021 (d) 84.9

8. Circle the number in which 7 has the value 0.000007

(a) 2.17 (b) 305.820967

(c) 51.74 (d) 497.392

Follow the example and write each decimal into a fraction or mixed number.

Example:

(a) 14.5 → $14\frac{5}{10}$ (b) 0.9 → $\frac{9}{10}$

Write each fraction or mixed number as decimal.

Example:

(a) $\frac{3}{10} \rightarrow 0.3$ (b) $13\frac{7}{10} \rightarrow 13.7$

Write the fraction or mixed number, the decimal number and the decimal word name where required.

Decimal number	Word name	Fraction or mixed number
0.5	five tenths	________
________	one and two tenths	$1\frac{2}{10}$
3.7	________	________
________	one tenth	________
________	________	$9\frac{7}{10}$

10.3 ________ ________

________ thirteen and nine tenths ________

________ ________ $\frac{6}{10}$

9.4 ________ ________

________ eighteen and two tenths ________

________ ________ $5\frac{8}{10}$

Write the decimal number and fraction shown in each picture. One has been done for you.

(a)

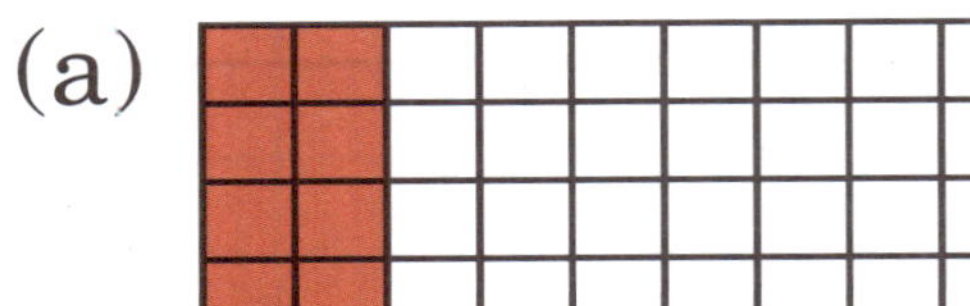

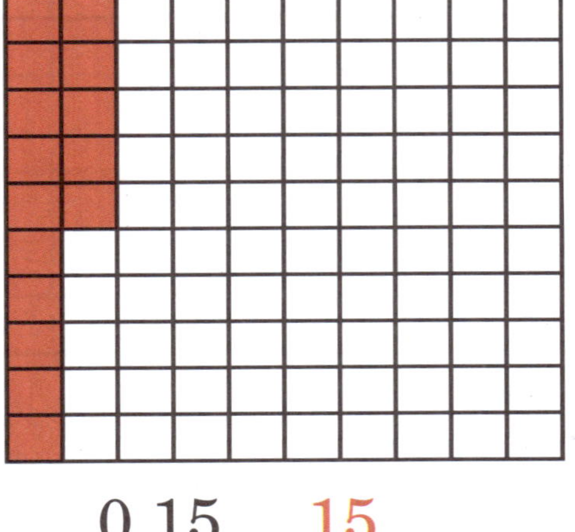

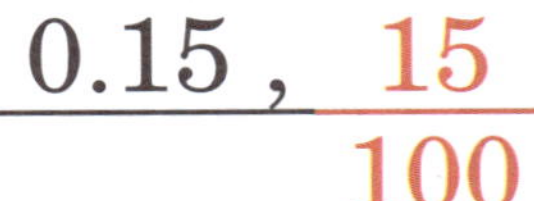

0.15 , $\frac{15}{100}$

(b)

(c)

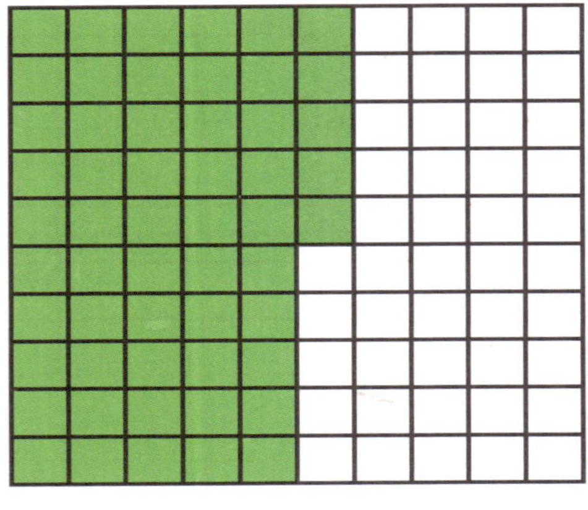

(d)

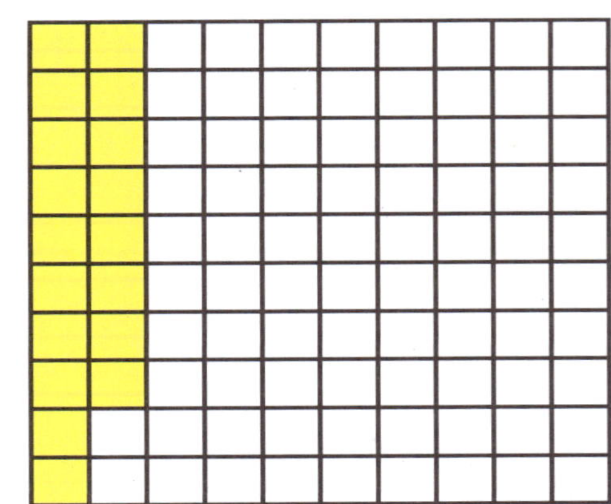

(e)

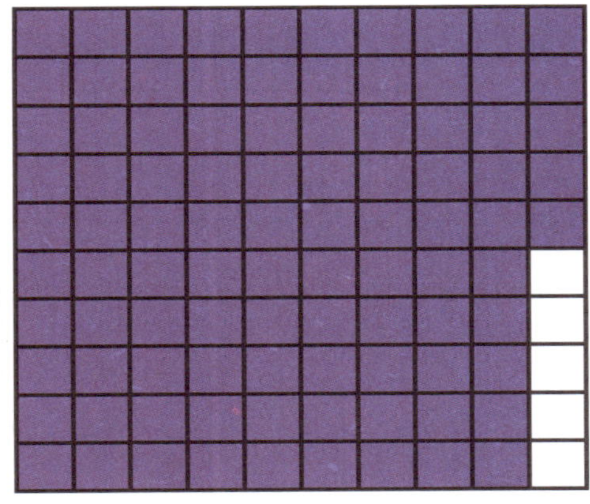

(f)

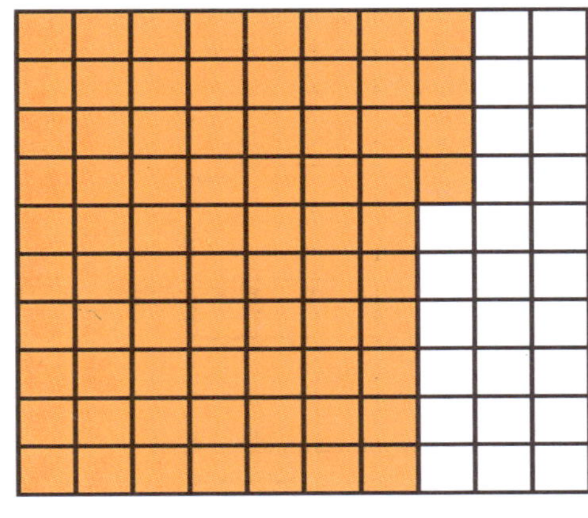

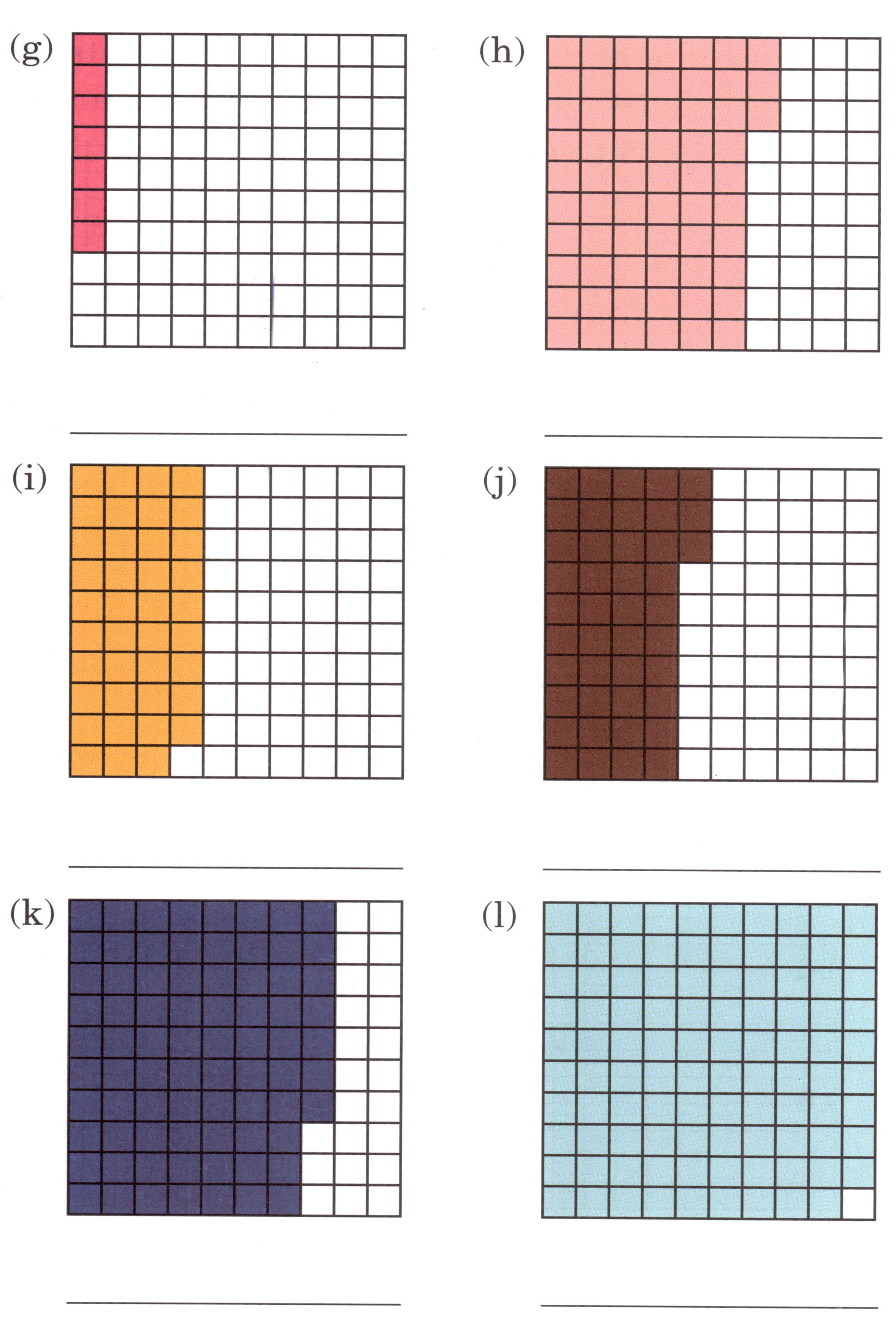
(g)
(h)
(i)
(j)
(k)
(l)

Each segment of the number line is divided into ten equal parts. Each part represents a decimal.

For example: 8.4 represented on a number line

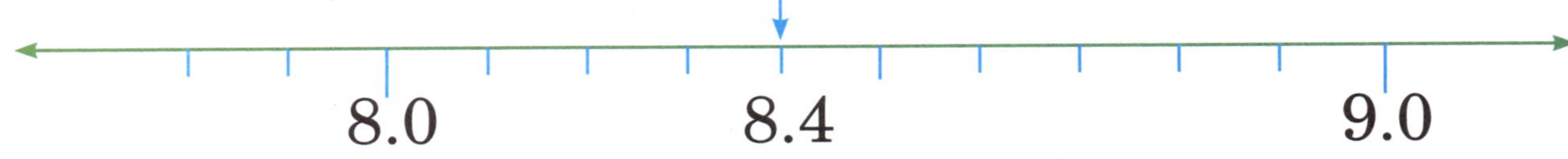

The arrow is four parts to the right of 8 where it points at 8.4.

Write the correct alphabet corresponding to the decimal numbers given below.

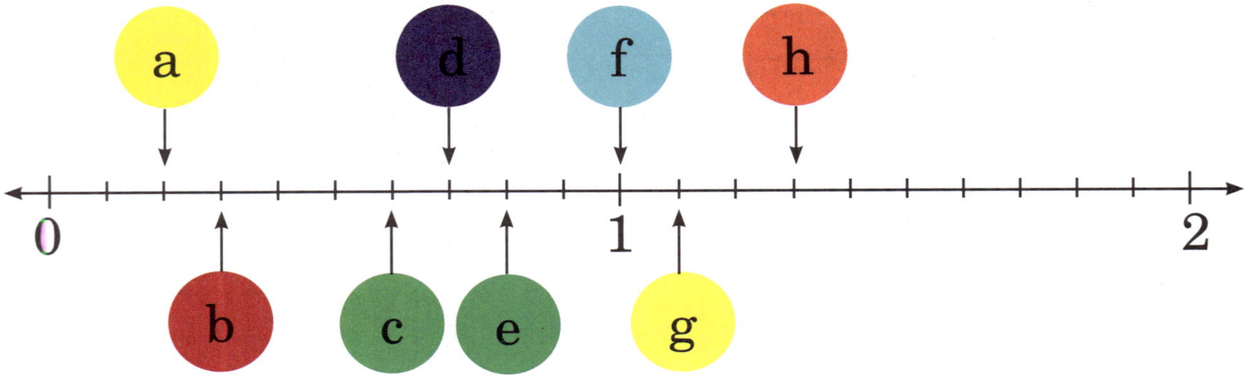

0.2 ______________ 0.3 ______________

0.6 ______________ 0.7 ______________

0.8 ______________ 1.0 ______________

1.1 ______________ 1.3 ______________

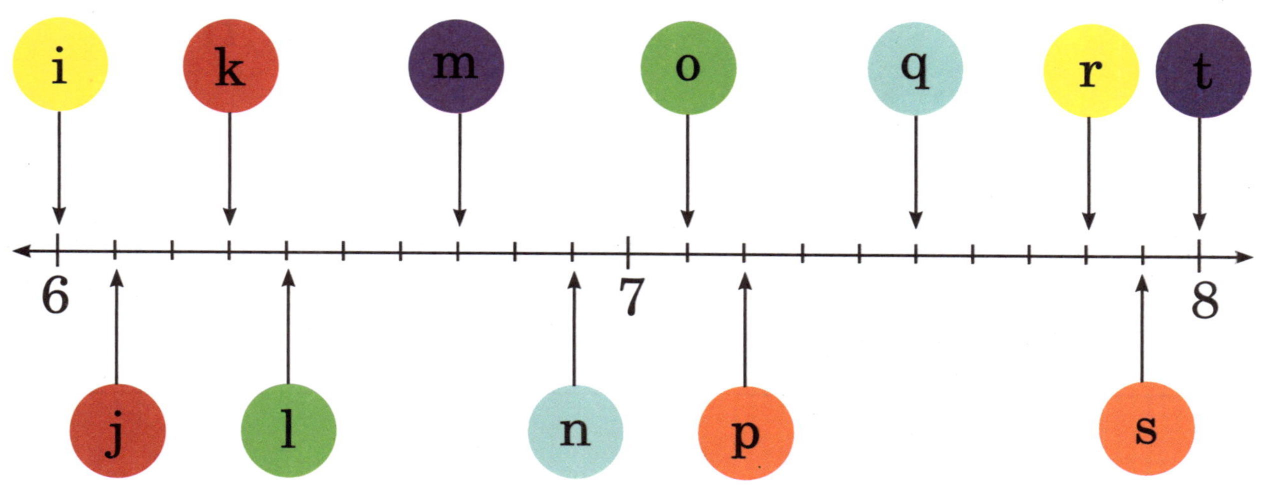

6.0	__________	6.1	__________
6.3	__________	6.4	__________
6.7	__________	6.9	__________
7.1	__________	7.2	__________
7.5	__________	7.8	__________
7.9	__________	8.0	__________

Rewrite the numbers in the order from the greatest to smallest.

4.5 4.05 5.4 5.45 5

____

3.2 3 2.03 2.02 2.23

____

6.02 6.3 5.1 6 6.2

____

9.08 4.05 98.1 9.8 9.88

____

2.1 6.5 11.8 10.2 11

____

8.8 5.6 3.6 7.1 7.6

____

7.29	7.9	9.7	6.2	5.9
5.3	6.3	3.6	9.3	3.5
18.423	19.2	18.432	18.21	19.6
2.02	2.012	2.021	2.01	2.018
9.6	8	9.9	8.8	8.4
22.021	22.102	22.012	22.201	22.042
10.38	7.83	10.32	7.23	8.24

Write the following decimals in words.

173.564 ____________________

2.35 ____________________

51.032 ____________________

45.2 ____________________

6.101 ____________________

84.67 ____________________

7.8 ____________________

368.90 ____________________

Write the following decimals in words.

267.5763 ____________________

93.720304 ____________________

5.9327 ____________________

80.41 ____________________

164.19041 ____________________

7.062 ____________________

31.25869 ____________________

472.834087 ____________________

Identify and write down the place value of the respective numbers.

1. Write down the place value of 7 in each of these numbers.

   (a) 78.924531 ______________________

   (b) 241.35708 ______________________

   (c) 9.7102 ______________________

   (d) 54.63817 ______________________

2. Write down the place value of 3 in each of these numbers.

   (a) 3.59216 ______________________

   (b) 47.2603 ______________________

   (c) 509.683 ______________________

   (d) 81.437659 ______________________

3. Write down the place value of 6 in each of these numbers.

   (a) 760.42183 ______________________

   (b) 3.189267 ______________________

   (c) 6.27 ______________________

   (d) 49.53768 ______________________

4. Write down the place value of 1 in each of these numbers.

(a) 278.15346 ____________________

(b) 19.36728 ____________________

(c) 352.901 ____________________

(d) 61.5429 ____________________

5. Write down the place value of 4 in each of these numbers.

(a) 4.19562 ____________________

(b) 38.403186 ____________________

(c) 13.82745 ____________________

(d) 479.65 ____________________

6. Write down the place value of 8 in each of these numbers.

(a) 9.72841 ____________________

(b) 28.5409 ____________________

(c) 463.187 ____________________

(d) 1.4538 ____________________

Let's us now learn to add decimals. While adding decimal numbers, it is important to line up the decimal points of the numbers that have to be added.

Write the numbers vertically just like we normally do for addition. You can add zeros to make the right side of the decimal points of the same length.

For example : 1.452 + 1.3

Step 1	Step 2	Step 3
1.452 + 1.3	1.452 + 1.300	1.452 + 1.300 2.752

Now perform addition for the following decimal numbers.

(a)
$$\begin{array}{r} 3.4 \\ +\ 5.7 \\ \hline \\ \hline \end{array}$$

(b)
$$\begin{array}{r} 0.4 \\ +\ 2.1 \\ \hline \\ \hline \end{array}$$

(c)
$$\begin{array}{r} 1.7 \\ +\ 9.8 \\ \hline \\ \hline \end{array}$$

(d)
$$\begin{array}{r} 2.5 \\ +\ 6.0 \\ \hline \\ \hline \end{array}$$

(e)
$$\begin{array}{r} 8.9 \\ +\ 4.75 \\ \hline \\ \hline \end{array}$$

(f)
$$\begin{array}{r} 4.1 \\ +\ 0.6 \\ \hline \\ \hline \end{array}$$

(g)
$$\begin{array}{r} 7.3 \\ +\ 5.23 \\ \hline \\ \hline \end{array}$$

(h)
$$\begin{array}{r} 2.8 \\ +\ 6.3 \\ \hline \\ \hline \end{array}$$

(i)
$$\begin{array}{r} 1.56 \\ +\ 4.7 \\ \hline \\ \hline \end{array}$$

(j)
$$\begin{array}{r} 0.9 \\ +\ 6.3 \\ \hline \\ \hline \end{array}$$

(k)
$$\begin{array}{r} 9.78 \\ +\ 7.0 \\ \hline \\ \hline \end{array}$$

(l)
$$\begin{array}{r} 0.31 \\ +\ 2.4 \\ \hline \\ \hline \end{array}$$

Add the following decimals.

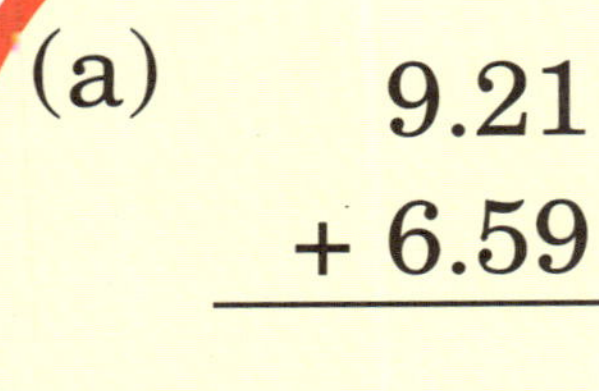

(a)
$$\begin{array}{r} 9.21 \\ +\ 6.59 \\ \hline \\ \hline \end{array}$$

(b)
$$\begin{array}{r} 2.51 \\ +\ 6.2 \\ \hline \\ \hline \end{array}$$

(c)
$$\begin{array}{r} 7.97 \\ +\ 8.26 \\ \hline \\ \hline \end{array}$$

(d)
$$\begin{array}{r} 8.93 \\ +\ 0.29 \\ \hline \\ \hline \end{array}$$

(e)
$$\begin{array}{r} 5.21 \\ +\ 8.6 \\ \hline \\ \hline \end{array}$$

(f)
$$\begin{array}{r} 5.11 \\ +\ 8.22 \\ \hline \\ \hline \end{array}$$

(g)
$$\begin{array}{r} 5.99 \\ +\ 4.3 \\ \hline \\ \hline \end{array}$$

(h)
$$\begin{array}{r} 8.37 \\ +\ 3.07 \\ \hline \\ \hline \end{array}$$

(i)
$$\begin{array}{r} 8.83 \\ +\ 8.16 \\ \hline \\ \hline \end{array}$$

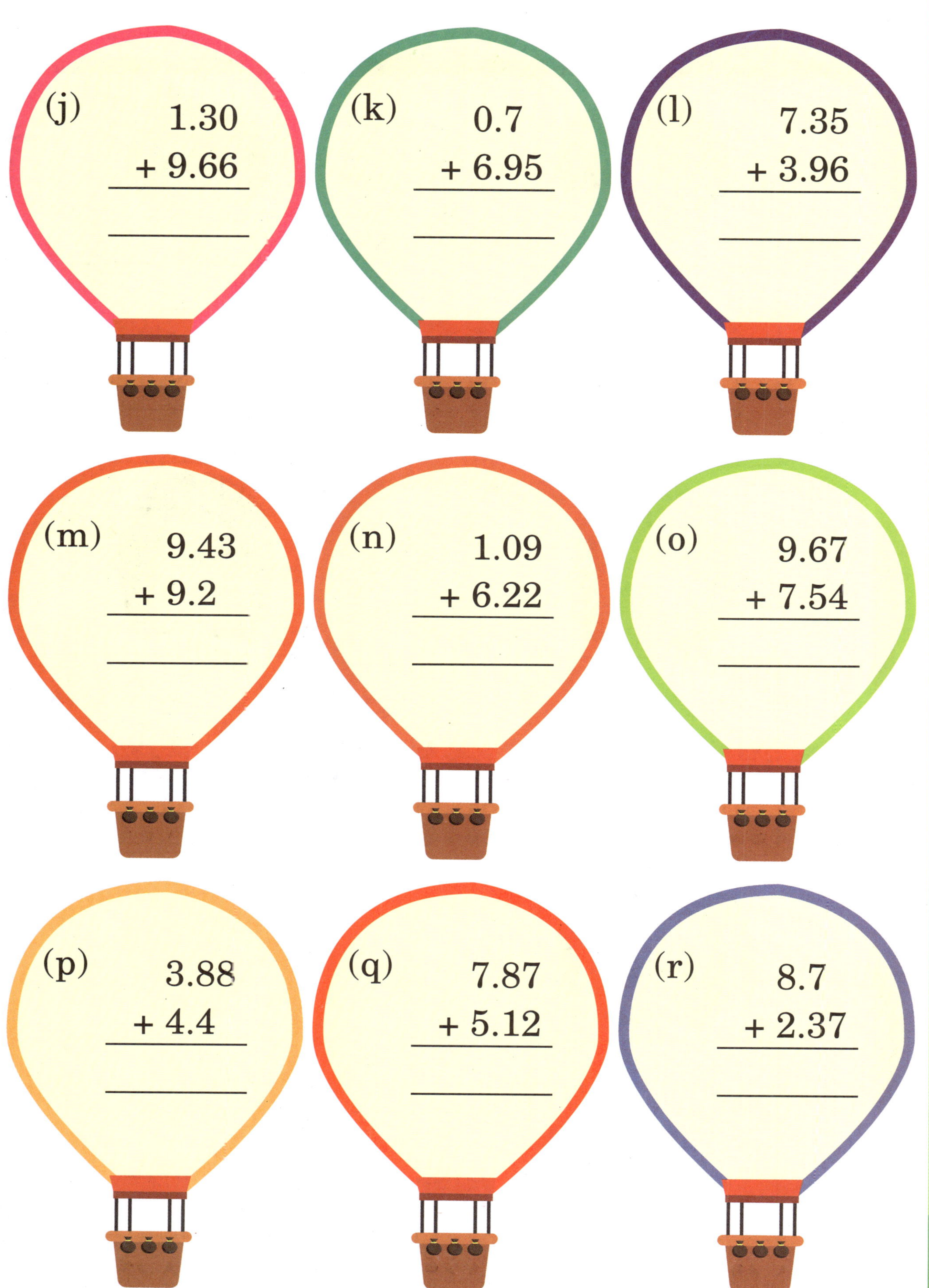

(j) 1.30 + 9.66 = ______

(k) 0.7 + 6.95 = ______

(l) 7.35 + 3.96 = ______

(m) 9.43 + 9.2 = ______

(n) 1.09 + 6.22 = ______

(o) 9.67 + 7.54 = ______

(p) 3.88 + 4.4 = ______

(q) 7.87 + 5.12 = ______

(r) 8.7 + 2.37 = ______

Add three decimals together.

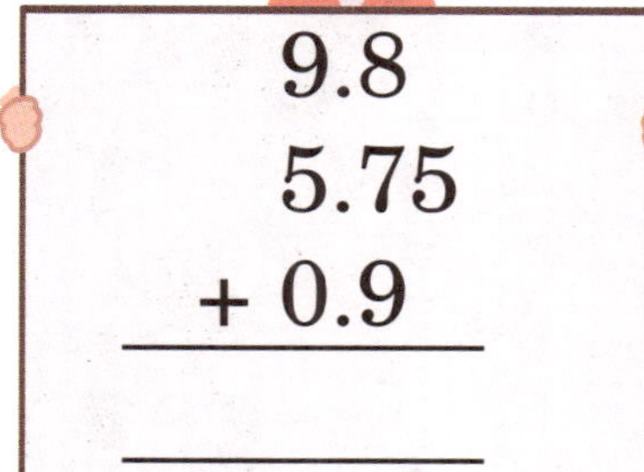

$$\begin{array}{r} 9.8 \\ 5.75 \\ +\ 0.9 \\ \hline \\ \hline \end{array}$$

$$\begin{array}{r} 4.9 \\ 2.5 \\ +\ 3.2 \\ \hline \\ \hline \end{array}$$

$$\begin{array}{r} 2.8 \\ 1.581 \\ +\ 3.3 \\ \hline \\ \hline \end{array}$$

$$\begin{array}{r} 8.2 \\ 0.6 \\ +\ 3.6 \\ \hline \\ \hline \end{array}$$

$$\begin{array}{r} 5.5 \\ 2.3 \\ +\ 7.2 \\ \hline \\ \hline \end{array}$$

$$\begin{array}{r} 2.625 \\ 0.6 \\ +\ 1.5 \\ \hline \\ \hline \end{array}$$

It is now time for subtraction! Subtracting decimals is the same as adding decimals. It is important to line up the decimal points of the numbers. Add zeros to the right and left side of the decimal point to make the numbers of the same length.

$$\begin{array}{r} 8.3 \\ -\ 3.6 \\ \hline \end{array}$$

$$\begin{array}{r} 9.6 \\ -\ 4.7 \\ \hline \end{array}$$

$$\begin{array}{r} 2.3 \\ -\ 1.8 \\ \hline \end{array}$$

$$\begin{array}{r} 7.4 \\ -\ 6.1 \\ \hline \end{array}$$

$$\begin{array}{r} 6.7 \\ -\ 3.4 \\ \hline \end{array}$$

$$\begin{array}{r} 4.4 \\ -\ 0.7 \\ \hline \end{array}$$

5.4
– 3.9

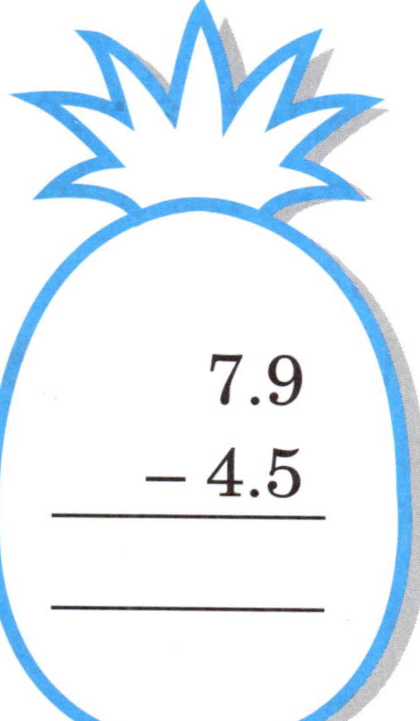
7.9
– 4.5

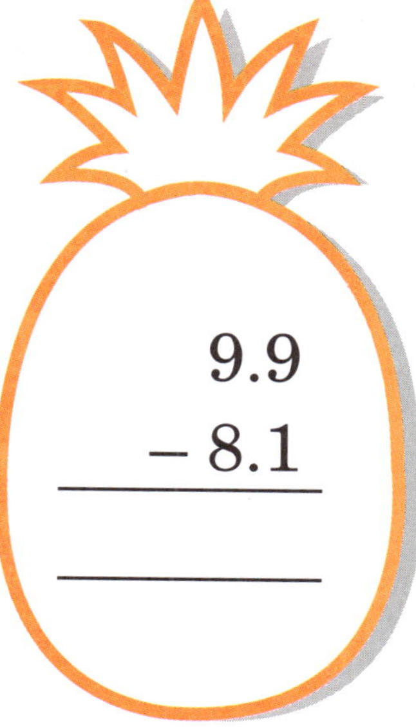
9.9
– 8.1

6.6
– 3.9

9.3
– 6.4

5.9
– 2.5

9.4
– 1.5

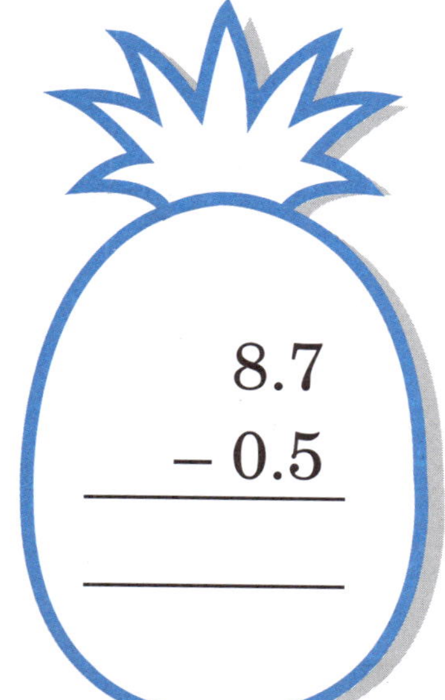
8.7
– 0.5

7.6
– 2.8

Subtract the following hundredths decimals.

7.85
– 4.08
9.27
– 3.64
3.14
– 0.07
7.3
– 4.92
2.27
– 1.54
7.56
– 4.6
8.6
– 5.12
7.24
– 1.2
8.98
– 4.28
9.42
– 5.21
8.57
– 5.43
4.32
– 3.21

Subtract the following hundredths decimals.

  0.139
– 0.023
____

____

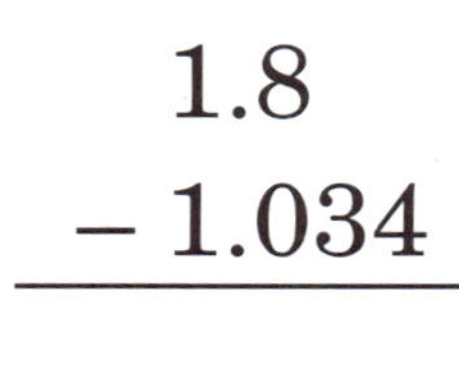

  1.8
– 1.034
____

____

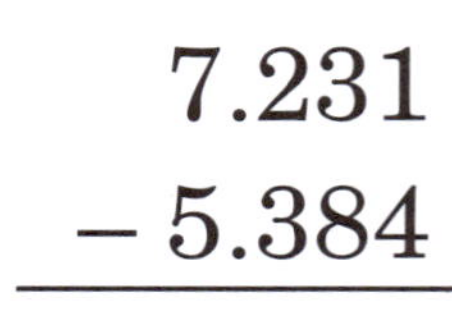

  7.231
– 5.384
____

____

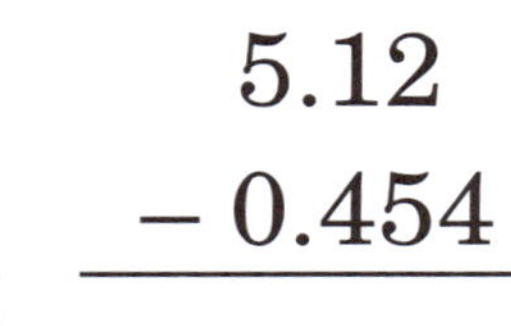

  5.12
– 0.454
____

____

  4.492
– 2.873
____

____

  3.23
– 0.009
____

____

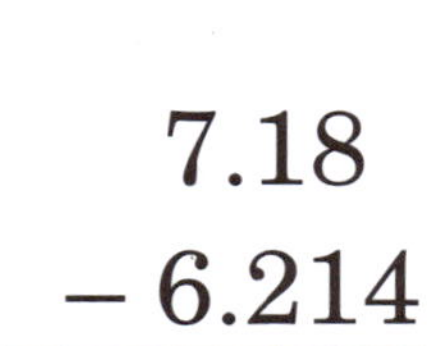

  7.18
– 6.214
____

____

  9.978
– 7.325
____

____

  2.034
– 1.4
____

____

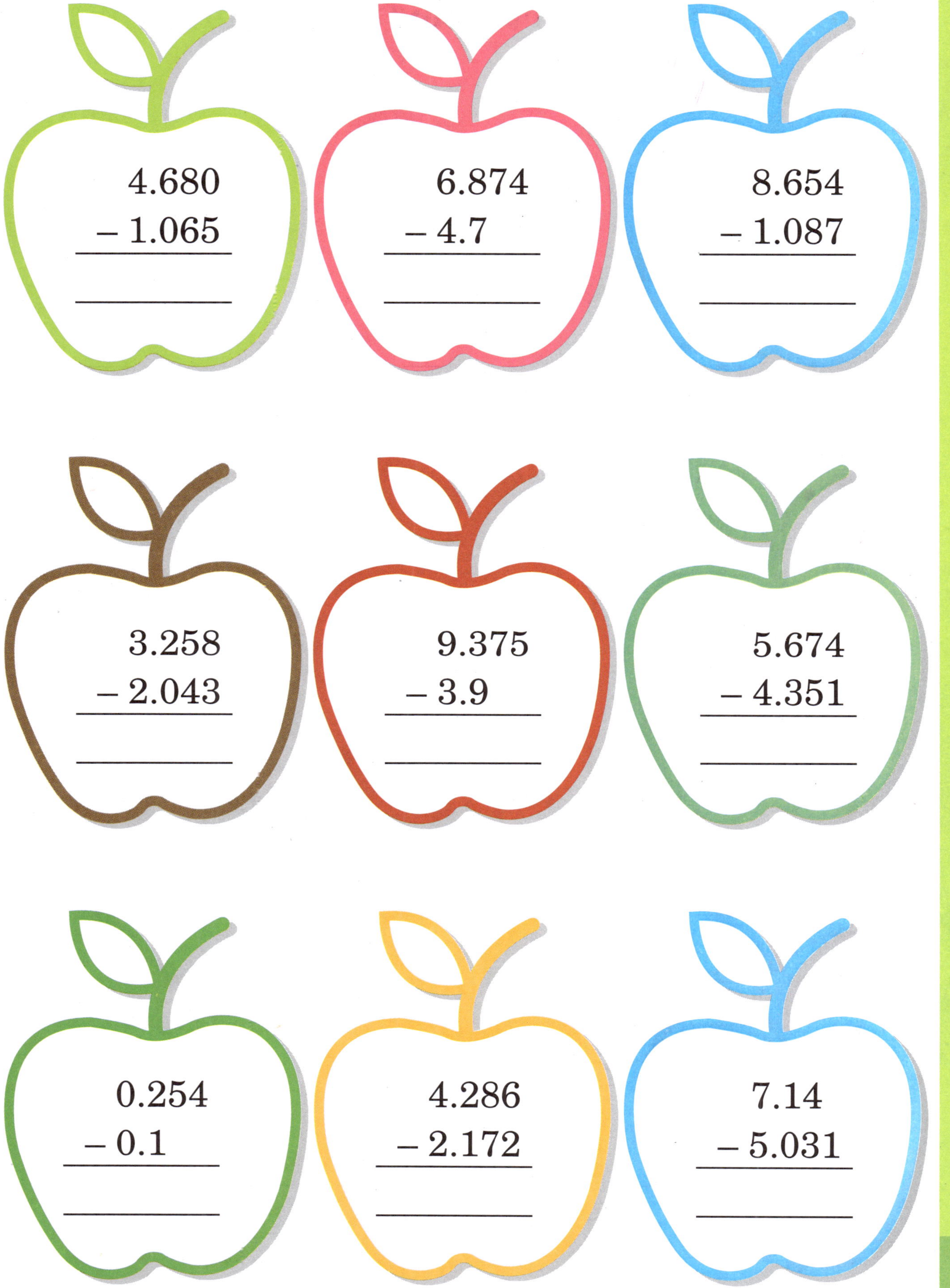
4.680
– 1.065
6.874
– 4.7
8.654
– 1.087
3.258
– 2.043
9.375
– 3.9
5.674
– 4.351
0.254
– 0.1
4.286
– 2.172
7.14
– 5.031

Solve the decimal problems given below.

334.62
– 210.52

402.85
+ 612.31

877.84
– 633.36

506.45
+ 816.75

987.41
– 689.37

249.52
+ 182.75

810.45
– 552.47

357.26
+ 159.67

Here are some decimal word problems. Read carefully and write the correct answer.

1. Neil and Jill plan to buy a gift for their mother. Jill has saved up $57.75 and Jenna $42 from their pocket money. How much money do they have in total to buy a present?

____

2. A box of chocolates contains 13.61 ounces of dark chocolate and 23.23 ounces of milk chocolate. How much do the chocolates weigh in total?

____

3. A group of friends visited a fruit farm on a holiday. They picked 10.34 pounds of oranges and 7.56 pounds of strawberries. How many pounds of fruits did they pick from the farm?

____

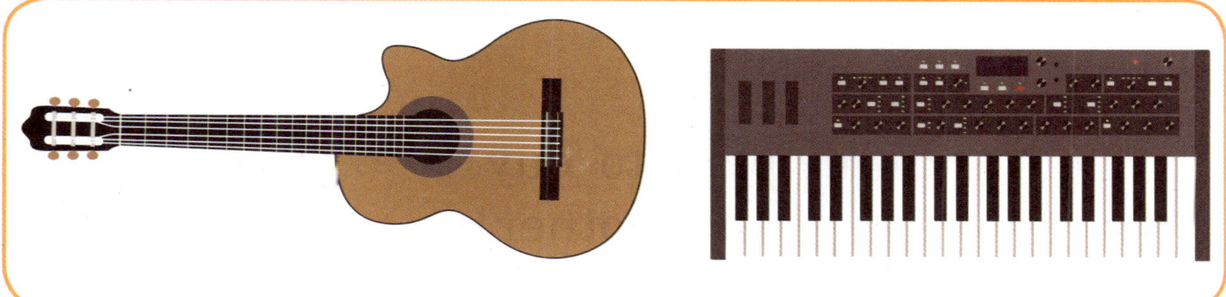

4. A man ordered a keyboard for $79.99 and an electric guitar for $54.99 for his twin sons. How much money did he spend in total on the musical instruments?

____

5. A group of college friends went on a road trip in a van. They stopped the van at the gas station after 56.7 miles to fill the tank. They reached their destination after driving for another 80.37 miles. How much distance did they cover to reach the destination?

____

1. Jack's dad spent $115.56 on groceries for a family dinner. He usually spends $36.91. How much more money did Jack's dad spend on groceries for the family dinner?

____

2. At the school clinic, the nurse measures Nick and Jane's height for a medical exam. Nick is 4.01 feet tall and Jane is 5.1 feet tall. How much taller is Jane than Nick?

____

3. Jim has decided to join the football team. But he needs to lose excess weight. He weighed 174.76 pounds before he started working out in the gym. He weighed 159.34 pounds after losing his weight. How many pounds did Jim lose?

____

4. At a camping trip, the forest officer tells kids that the tallest tree situated in the forest is 342.7 feet. Earlier the tallest tree of the forest was 326.77 feet. What is the difference between the height of the two trees?

____

5. Ally takes a bus to her grandmother's house, which is 190.8 miles away from her home. She drives 97.7 miles and stops at a nearby motel. How many more miles does Ally need to drive, to reach her grandmother's house?

____

6. Ella is eating a chocolate bar with 22 pieces. She has finished eating 9.5 pieces. Ella's sister Zoey takes the remaining chocolate to eat it herself. How much chocolate is left for Zoey? ______________________

Solve the combination of subtraction problems and write the correct answer.

$$\begin{array}{r} 7.5 \\ -\ 2.3 \\ \hline \end{array}$$

$$\begin{array}{r} 8.6 \\ -\ 7.9 \\ \hline \end{array}$$

$$\begin{array}{r} 4.3 \\ -\ 1.7 \\ \hline \end{array}$$

$$\begin{array}{r} 5.4 \\ -\ 0.8 \\ \hline \end{array}$$

$$\begin{array}{r} 5.1 \\ -\ 4.3 \\ \hline \end{array}$$

$$\begin{array}{r} 6.7 \\ -\ 3.4 \\ \hline \end{array}$$

$$\begin{array}{r} 9.7 \\ -\ 8.3 \\ \hline \end{array}$$

$$\begin{array}{r} 1.4 \\ -\ 0.2 \\ \hline \end{array}$$

$$\begin{array}{r} 7.4 \\ -\ 4.6 \\ \hline \end{array}$$

$7.2 - 6.3 =$ ☐

$3.9 - 1.2 =$ ☐

$8.1 - 3.7 =$ ☐

$4.8 - 3.1 =$ ☐

$2.2 - 1.7 =$ ☐

$7.6 - 6.4 =$ ☐

$6.2 - 4.4 =$ ☐

$5.2 - 1.6 =$ ☐

$3.5 - 0.8 =$ ☐

$8.5 - 6.5 =$ ☐

$7.2 - 4.1 =$ ☐

Solve the decimals sums given below.

621.75
+ 234.86
71.92
+ 84.35
43.91
+ 521.3
90.4
+ 418.53
521.3
+ 152.47
675.52
+ 97.6

1. A city recorded its tallest building at 602.1 metres. It's shortest building was 150.63 metres long. Calculate the difference in the height of the two buildings.

____

2. Mason goes to shop and buys many things. He purchases items worth $79.99 and $51.99. How much money did Mason spend?

____

3. Helen bought a magazine subscription of $81.63 annually. But she had to pay only $56 after using a discount coupon. How much money did Helen save?

____

4. Gale used 8.74 cm of ribbon to fix her ballet shoes. She bought another 12.32 cm of ribbon to make a matching bow. How much ribbon did Gale use in total?

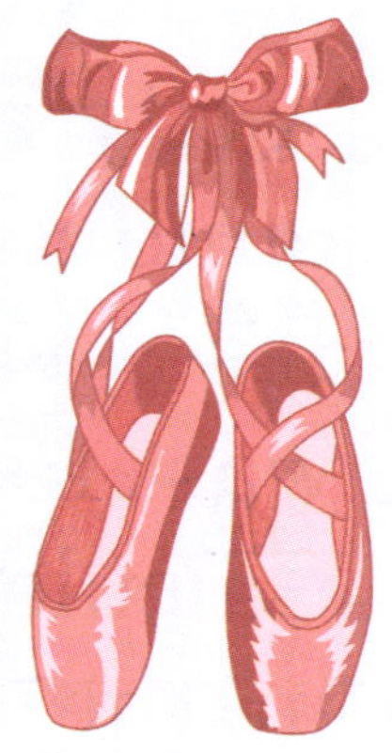

____

5. Lisa's family owns two cars. The fuel tank capacity of the red car is 22.45 gallons. The blue car can hold about 8.7 gallons of fuel. How much more fuel can be stored in the red car than the blue car?

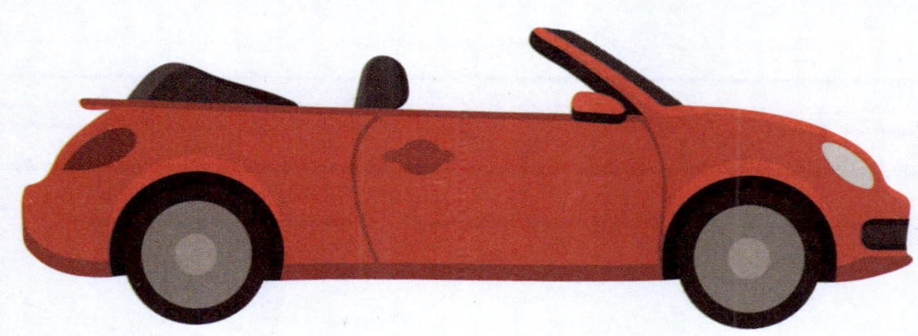

____

6. Betty went to the supermarket to buy ingredients to bake a cake. She bought 300 grams of flour, 17.65 grams of vanilla essence, 5.5 grams of baking soda and 3 eggs. What is the total weight of all the ingredients that Betty bought? ____________________

Mark the alphabets on the number line for each decimal point.

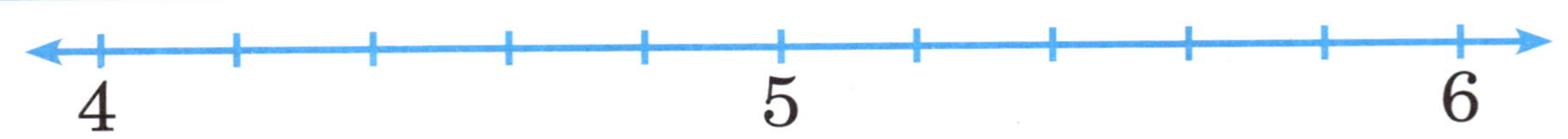

A = <u>4.6</u> B = <u>4.2</u> C = <u>5.4</u> D = <u>5.8</u>

2 3 4

A = <u>2.2</u> B = <u>3.4</u> C = <u>2.6</u> D = <u>3.8</u>

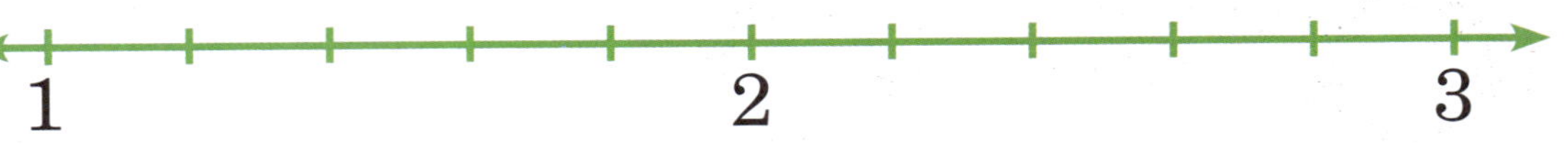

A = <u>1.4</u> B = <u>2.6</u> C = <u>2.8</u> D = <u>1.2</u>

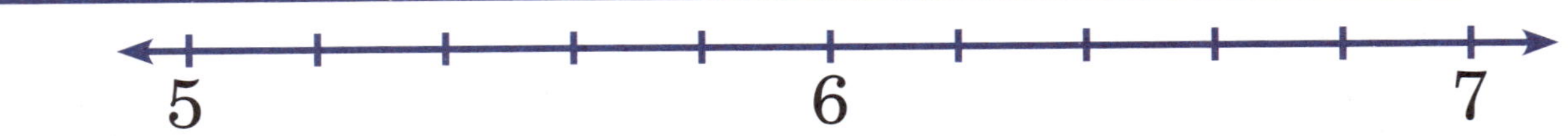

A = <u>6.6</u> B = <u>5.4</u> C = <u>5.2</u> D = <u>6.8</u>

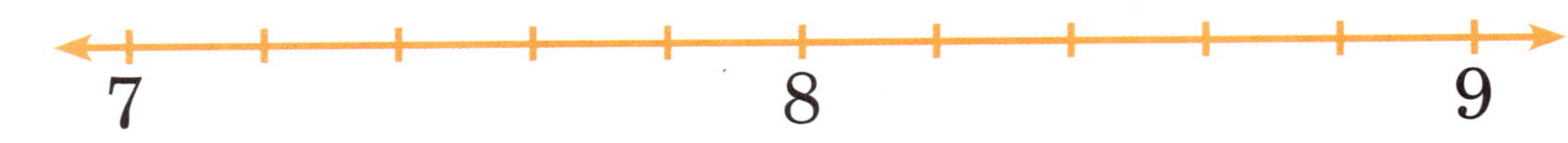

A = <u>7.6</u> B = <u>7.8</u> C = <u>8.2</u> D = <u>8.8</u>